Dirty Air

by Ellen Lawrence

Consultants:

Ann M. Dillner, PhD
IMPROVE Group, University of California, Davis

Kimberly Brenneman, PhD
National Institute for Early Education Research, Rutgers University
New Brunswick, New Jersey

BEARPORT PUBLISHING

New York, New York

Credits

Cover, © Tom Wang/Shutterstock, © Antonov Roman/Shutterstock, © ssuaphotos/Shutterstock, and © Image Source/Corbis; 2–3, © Michal Kodym/Istock/Thinkstock; 4, © Hurst Photo/Shutterstock; 4–5, © Hung Chung Chih/Shutterstock; 6, © wrangler/Shutterstock; 7, © Kekyalyaynen/Shutterstock; 8–9, © Ranglen/Shutterstock; 10, © Verkhovynets Taras/Shutterstock; II, © Paulo Manuel Furtado Pires/iStock/Thinkstock; 12, © bikeriderlondon/Shutterstock; 13, © TonyV3112/Shutterstock; 14, © Ryan McGinnis/Alamy; 15, © Mary Terriberry/Shutterstock; 15T, © Volodymyr Goinyk/Shutterstock; 16, © Monkey Business Images/Shutterstock; 17TL, © Tupungato/Shutterstock; 17BL, © Rudy Balasko/Shutterstock; 17R, © spotmatik/Shutterstock; 18T, © Sue Cunningham Photographic/Alamy; 18B, © Liufuyu/Istock/Thinkstock; 19, © manfredxy/Istock/Thinkstock; 20, © Wessel du Plooy/Shutterstock; 21TL, © Tetra Images/Alamy; 21TC, © Istock/Thinkstock; 21TR, © Anne Kitzman/Shutterstock; 21B, © Sebastien Burel/Shutterstock; 22, © Timolina/Shutterstock, © TigerForce/Shutterstock, © Adam Gryko/Shutterstock, and © Gouraud Studio/Shutterstock; 23, © Alicar/Shutterstock, © Jacek Chabraszewski/Shutterstock, and © Verkhovynets Taras/Shutterstock.

Publisher: Kenn Goin
Creative Director: Spencer Brinker
Design: Emma Randall
Editor: Mark J. Sachner
Photo Researcher: Ruby Tuesday Books Ltd

Library of Congress Cataloging-in-Publication Data

Lawrence, Ellen, 1967– author.
  Dirty air / by Ellen Lawrence.
      pages cm — (Green world, clean world)
  Includes bibliographical references and index.
  ISBN-13: 978-1-62724-103-8 (library binding)
  ISBN-10: 1-62724-103-5 (library binding)
 1. Air—Pollution—Juvenile literature. 2. Air—Pollution—Environmental aspects—Juvenile literature.
3. Air—Pollution—Health aspects—Juvenile literature. I. Title.
  TD883.13.L374 2014
  363.739'2—dc23
                                    2013045451

For more information, write to Bearport Publishing Company, Inc., 45 West 21st Street, Suite 3B, New York, New York 10010. Printed in the United States of America.

10 9 8 7 6 5 4 3 2 1

Contents

Dangerous Air

It's morning in a busy city.

Thousands of cars carry people to work and school.

Hundreds of trucks make deliveries to homes and businesses.

These vehicles make life easier for people, but they can also make our air dirty. How?

In a notebook, keep a record of how many times you travel in a car or bus in one week.

Sometimes the air looks smoky or smells bad when it is dirty. Often, though, gases and other kinds of **pollution** in the air are invisible and have no smell.

Burning Fuel

Most vehicles are powered by gasoline or diesel.

These fuels are made from oil.

When fuels made from oil are burned in a vehicle's engine, harmful **gases** are released.

Tiny **particles** of **chemicals** and **soot** are released, too.

This pollution is harmful to people and to the **environment**.

It spreads everywhere as it floats in the air.

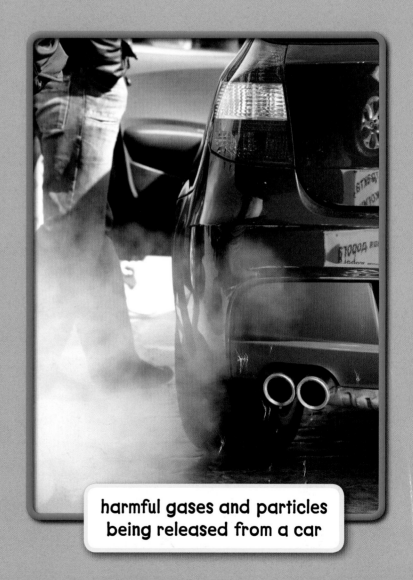

harmful gases and particles being released from a car

When fuels made from oil are burned, a gas called carbon dioxide is released. Too much carbon dioxide in the air traps the sun's heat on Earth and helps cause **global warming**.

Making Electricity

Driving vehicles is not the only way harmful gases and particles get in the air.

Power plants that make electricity also cause pollution.

These plants use coal and **natural gas** to make **energy**.

When these fuels are burned, they release pollution into the air.

Every day, we use a lot of electricity. Whenever we turn on a light or a computer, electricity is being used.

Pollution All Around

People can cause air pollution in other ways, too.

Anything that releases smoke and dust makes the air dirty.

When buildings are built or torn down, lots of dust is stirred up.

When wildfires burn forests, smoke and ash fill the air.

The wind moves all of this polluted air from place to place.

dust

Smoke from outdoor barbecues, indoor fireplaces, and wood-burning stoves all pollute the air.

Health Effects

To be healthy, people need to breathe clean air.

Spending time in polluted air can make them sick.

It can hurt their eyes and make them cough.

Dirty air can also cause diseases, such as **asthma,** that make it hard to breathe.

If people with asthma breathe polluted air, they may become very ill.

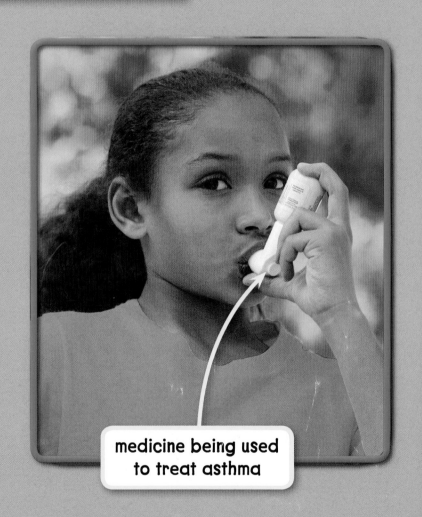

medicine being used to treat asthma

mask

Sometimes when the air is dirty, people wear masks. The masks help stop them from breathing in polluted air.

Acid Rain

Air pollution isn't only bad for people, it's also harmful in another way.

When poisonous gases float up into the sky, they mix with raindrops in clouds.

This creates **acid rain**.

When acid rain falls on trees and other plants, it can kill them.

Acid rain also poisons rivers and lakes, killing the animals and plants that live in them.

a statue damaged by acid rain

Acid rain can even damage buildings and statues made of stone. Over time, the rain causes parts of the stone to crumble and fall off.

healthy pine trees

pine trees killed
by acid rain

What do you think
people can do to
stop air pollution?

Reducing Air Pollution

How people choose to travel can help reduce air pollution.

For example, traveling by bus or by train is better than using a car.

Trains and buses can carry many more riders than cars.

That means the amount of pollution produced to carry each passenger is much less.

When people travel by walking or bicycling, they produce no pollution at all!

take a bus

ride a train

ride a bike

17

Making Cleaner Electricity

People can also help reduce air pollution by making electricity without burning fuel.

Hydroelectric power uses the flow of water to make electricity.

Wind power uses the wind's energy to make electricity.

Solar power captures the sun's light to make electricity.

hydroelectric power

wind power

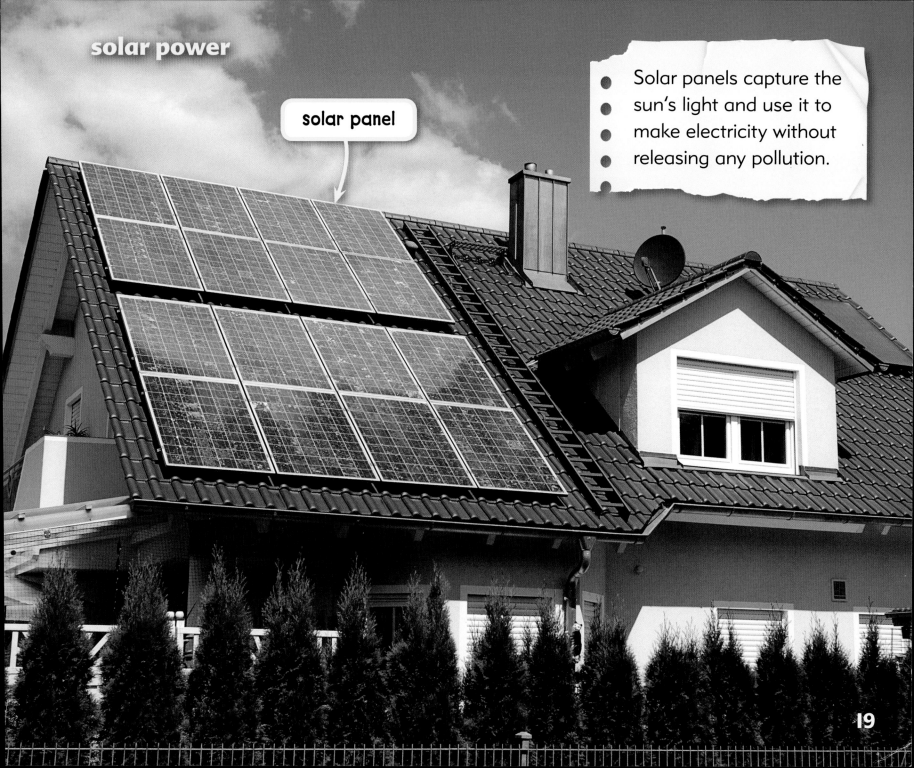

Be a Clean Air Champion!

Reducing how much electricity you use can help make the air cleaner.

When you turn off a light or computer, you use less electricity.

When lots of people use less electricity, power plants burn less fuel.

Then fewer harmful gases are released into the air.

By using less electricity, we make the air cleaner for everyone!

regular lightbulb

energy-saving lightbulb

- Use energy-saving lightbulbs. These bulbs use less electricity than regular bulbs and they last longer!

How to Cut Air Pollution

Carpool to school whenever possible. Energy is saved when friends share a ride instead of taking separate cars.

On hot days, close curtains and shades. That will keep out the sun's heat and reduce the amount of air conditioning you need.

Only run the dishwasher when it's full of dishes. It takes as much energy to run a half-empty dishwasher as one that is full.

Many trucks travel hundreds of miles to carry food from where it is grown to where it is sold. Driving these long distances burns lots of fuel, which produces air pollution. You can save energy and reduce pollution by buying fruits and vegetables grown close to your home.

Science Lab

Acid Rain Experiment

Discover what acid does to plants by making your own acid rain from lemon juice and water. Lemons contain a type of acid called citric acid, which gives them their sour taste.

You will need:

- A measuring cup
- One cup of lemon juice
- Three cups of water
- Three small jars with lids
- Sticky labels
- A marker
- Three small plants in pots
- A tablespoon
- A notebook and pencil

How to Set Up Your Experiment

1 Pour half a cup of lemon juice and half a cup of water into a jar. Label the jar A.

2 Pour a quarter of a cup of lemon juice and three-quarters of a cup of water into a second jar. Label this jar B.

3 Pour one cup of water into a third jar. Label this jar C.

4 Take three small potted plants and label them A, B, and C.

5 Put two tablespoons of liquid from jar A into plant A's pot. Put two tablespoons of liquid from jar B into plant B's pot. Finally, put two tablespoons of liquid from jar C into plant C's pot.

6 Every day for the next two to three weeks, give each plant two tablespoons of liquid from its jar.

What do you think will happen to plant A? How about plants B and C? In your notebook, write down your ideas.

Then keep a record of everything you observe happening to the plants. What did you notice?

(To learn more about this experiment, turn to page 24.)

Science Words

acid rain (ASS-id RAYN) a harmful type of rain that contains chemicals called acids; acid rain can be harmful to plants, animals, and buildings

asthma (AZ-muh) a medical condition that makes it difficult for people to breathe

chemicals (KEM-uh-kuhlz) natural or human-made substances that can sometimes be harmful to living things

energy (EN-ur-jee) power, such as electricity, that machines need in order to work

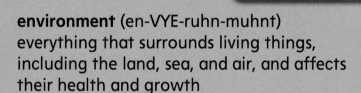

environment (en-VYE-ruhn-muhnt) everything that surrounds living things, including the land, sea, and air, and affects their health and growth

gases (GASS-iz) matter that floats in air and is neither a liquid nor a solid; most gases are invisible

global warming (GLOHB-uhl WARM-ing) the slow and steady heating up of Earth's air and oceans caused by certain gases that trap the sun's heat in Earth's atmosphere

hydroelectric power (*hye*-droh-i-LEK-trik POU-ur) electricity that is produced using moving water

natural gas (NACH-ur-uhl GASS) a type of fuel that is buried deep underground; it can be used to power stoves and heat homes

particles (PAR-tuh-kuhlz) tiny pieces of solid matter, such as dust or soot, or tiny liquid drops

pollution (puh-LOO-shuhn) materials, such as trash, chemicals, gases, and dust, that can damage the air, water, or soil

power plants (POU-ur PLANTS) large factories that produce electricity

soot (SUT) a black, dust-like powder that is made when something is burned

Index

Read More

Katz Cooper, Sharon. *Using Air (Exploring Earth's Resources).* Chicago: Heinemann (2007).

Minden, Cecilia. *Kids Can Keep Air Clean (21st Century Basic Skills Library).* Ann Arbor, MI: Cherry Lake (2011).

Learn More Online

To learn more about dirty air, visit
www.bearportpublishing.com/GreenWorldCleanWorld

About the Author

Ellen Lawrence lives in the United Kingdom. Her favorite books to write are those about nature and animals. In fact, the first book Ellen bought for herself, when she was six years old, was the story of a gorilla named Patty Cake that was born in New York's Central Park Zoo.

Science Lab (Page 22)

Plant A, which was given water with lots of acid in it, probably began to look unhealthy—and may have died. Plant B, which was given less acid than plant A, likely looked better than plant A. Plant C probably stayed healthy. That's because it wasn't given any acid.